W9-BEL-145

# Glad Tidings of Great Joy

# Glad Tidings of Great Joy

## CHRISTMAS AT THE ART INSTITUTE OF CHICAGO

·AIC·

©1993 by The Art Institute of Chicago

No portion of this publication may be reproduced in any manner whatsoever without prior permission in writing from The Art Institute of Chicago Publications Department 111 South Michigan Avenue, Chicago, Illinois 60603-6110

ISBN: 0-86559-123-7

Frontispiece:
*Virgin and Child with Angel* by Sandro Botticelli

Facing Page:
Detail of *The Adoration of the Eucharist* by Peter Paul Rubens

*For unto us a child is born,*
*unto us a son is given:*
*and the government*
*shall be upon his shoulder:*
*and his name shall be called*
*Wonderful, Counsellor,*
*The mighty God,*
*The everlasting Father,*
*The Prince of Peace.*

ISAIAH 9:6

THERE was in the days of Herod, the king of Judaea, a certain priest named Zacharias, of the course of Abia: and his wife was of the daughters of Aaron, and her name was Elisabeth.

And they were both righteous before God, walking in all the commandments and ordinances of the Lord blameless.

And they had no child, because that Elisabeth was barren, and they both were now well stricken in years.

And it came to pass, that while he executed the priest's office before God in the order of his course,

According to the custom of the priest's office, his lot was to burn incense when he went into the temple of the Lord.

And the whole multitude of the people were praying without at the time of incense.

And there appeared unto him an angel of the Lord standing on the right side of the altar of incense.

And when Zacharias saw him, he was troubled, and fear fell upon him.

But the angel said unto him, Fear not, Zacharias: for thy prayer is heard; and thy wife Elisabeth shall bear thee a son, and thou shalt call his name John.

And thou shalt have joy and gladness; and many shall rejoice at his birth.

And Zacharias said unto the angel, Whereby shall I know this? for I am an old man, and my wife well stricken in years.

And the angel answering said unto him, I am Gabriel, that stand in the presence of God; and am sent to speak unto thee and to shew thee these glad tidings.

And, behold, thou shalt be dumb, and not able to speak, until the day that these things shall be performed, because thou believest not my words, which shall be fulfilled in their season.

And the people waited for Zacharias, and marvelled that he tarried so long in the temple.

And when he came out, he could not speak unto them: and they perceived that he had seen a vision in the temple: for he beckoned unto them, and remained speechless.

And it came to pass, that, as soon as the days of his ministration were accomplished, he departed to his own house.

And after those days his wife Elisabeth conceived, and hid herself five months, saying,

Thus hath the Lord dealt with me in the days wherein he looked on me, to take away my reproach among men.

*The Annunciation* by Jean Hey (The Master of Moulins)

Aᴎᴅ in the sixth month the angel Gabriel was sent from God unto a city of Galilee, named Nazareth,

To a virgin espoused to a man whose name was Joseph, of the house of David; and the virgin's name was Mary.

And the angel came in unto her, and said, Hail, thou that art highly favoured, the Lord is with thee: blessed art thou among women.

And when she saw him, she was troubled at his saying, and cast in her mind what manner of salutation this should be.

And the angel said unto her, Fear not, Mary: for thou hast found favour with God.

And, behold, thou shalt conceive in thy womb, and bring forth a son, and shalt call his name JESUS.

He shall be great, and shall be called the Son of the Highest: and the Lord God shall give unto him the throne of his father David:

And he shall reign over the house of Jacob for ever; and of his kingdom there shall be no end.

Then said Mary unto the angel, How shall this be, seeing I know not a man?

And the angel answered and said unto her, The Holy Ghost shall come upon thee, and the power of the Highest shall overshadow thee: therefore also that holy thing which shall be born of thee shall be called the Son of God.

And, behold, thy cousin Elisabeth, she hath also conceived a son in her old age: and this is the sixth month with her, who was called barren.

For with God nothing shall be impossible.

And Mary said, Behold the handmaid of the Lord; be it unto me according to thy word. And the angel departed from her.

*The Annunciation*
by Johann Koerbecke

ＡND Mary arose in those days, and went into the hill country with haste, into a city of Juda;

And entered into the house of Zacharias, and saluted Elisabeth.

And it came to pass, that, when Elisabeth heard the salutation of Mary, the babe leaped in her womb; and Elisabeth was filled with the Holy Ghost:

And she spake out with a loud voice, and said, Blessed art thou among women, and blessed is the fruit of thy womb.

And whence is this to me, that the mother of my Lord should come to me?

For, lo, as soon as the voice of thy salutation sounded in mine ears, the babe leaped in my womb for joy.

And blessed is she that believed: for there shall be a performance of those things which were told her from the Lord.

And Mary said, My soul doth magnify the Lord, And my spirit hath rejoiced in God my Saviour.

For he hath regarded the low estate of his handmaiden: for, behold, from henceforth all generations shall call me blessed.

For he that is mighty hath done to me great things; and holy is his name.

And his mercy is on them that fear him from generation to generation.

He hath shewed strength with his arm; he hath scattered the proud in the imagination of their hearts.

He hath put down the mighty from their seats, and exalted them of low degree.

He hath filled the hungry with good things; and the rich he hath sent empty away.

He hath holpen his servant Israel, in remembrance of his mercy;

As he spake to our fathers, to Abraham, and to his seed for ever.

And Mary abode with her about three months, and returned to her own house.

The Visitation (detail)
from *Scenes from the Life of Saint John the Baptist*
by Bartolommeo di Giovanni

Now Elisabeth's full time came that she should be delivered; and she brought forth a son.

And her neighbours and her cousins heard how the Lord had shewed great mercy upon her; and they rejoiced with her.

And it came to pass, that on the eighth day they came to circumcise the child; and they called him Zacharias, after the name of his father.

And his mother answered and said, Not so; but he shall be called John.

*Scenes from the Life of Saint John the Baptist* by Bartolommeo di Giovanni

Aɴᴅ they said unto her, There is none of thy kindred that is called by this name.

And they made signs to his father, how he would have him called.

And he asked for a writing table, and wrote, saying, His name is John. And they marvelled all.

And his mouth was opened immediately, and his tongue loosed, and he spake, and praised God.

AND it came to pass in those days, that there went out a decree from Caesar Augustus, that all the world should be taxed.

And all went to be taxed, every one into his own city.

And Joseph also went up from Galilee, out of the city of Nazareth, into Judaea, unto the city of David, which is called Bethlehem; (because he was of the house and lineage of David:)

To be taxed with Mary his espoused wife, being great with child.

And so it was, that, while they were there, the days were accomplished that she should be delivered.

And she brought forth her firstborn son, and wrapped him in swaddling clothes, and laid him in a manger; because there was no room for them in the inn.

*The Nativity*
by Master of the Historia
Friderici et Maximiliani

AND there were in the
same country shepherds abiding in the field,
keeping watch over their flock by night.

And, lo, the angel of the Lord
came upon them, and the glory of the Lord
shone round about them: and they were
sore afraid.

And the angel said unto them,
Fear not: for, behold, I bring you good tidings
of great joy, which shall be to all
people.

For unto you is born this
day in the city of David a Saviour,
which is Christ the Lord.

And this shall be a sign
unto you; Ye shall find the babe
wrapped in swaddling clothes,
lying in a manger.

*The Annunciation*
*to the Shepherds*
from an anonymous
Book of Hours

AND suddenly there was with the angel a multitude of the heavenly host praising God,

AND saying, Glory to God in the highest, and on earth peace, good will toward men.

Aɴᴅ it came to pass, as the angels were gone away from them into heaven, the shepherds said one to another, Let us now go even unto Bethlehem, and see this thing which is come to pass, which the Lord hath made known unto us.

And they came with haste, and found Mary, and Joseph, and the babe lying in a manger.

And when they had seen it, they made known abroad the saying which was told them concerning this child.

And all they that heard it wondered at those things which were told them by the shepherds.

But Mary kept all these things, and pondered them in her heart.

And the shepherds returned, glorifying and praising God for all the things that they had heard and seen, as it was told unto them.

*The Adoration of the Christ Child*
by Jacob Cornelisz. van Oostsanen
(detail on pages 22-23)

A<small>ND</small> when eight days were accomplished for the circumcising of the child, his name was called J<small>ESUS</small>, which was so named of the angel before he was conceived in the womb.

And when the days of her purification according to the law of Moses were accomplished, they brought him to Jerusalem, to present him to the Lord;

And to offer a sacrifice according to that which is said in the law of the Lord, A pair of turtledoves, or two young pigeons.

And, behold, there was a man in Jerusalem, whose name was Simeon; and the same man was just and devout, waiting for the consolation of Israel: and the Holy Ghost was upon him.

And it was revealed unto him by the Holy Ghost, that he should not see death, before he had seen the Lord's Christ.

And he came by the Spirit into the temple: and when the parents brought in the child Jesus, to do for him after the custom of the law,

Then took he him up in his arms, and blessed God, and said,

Lord, now lettest thou thy servant depart in peace, according to thy word:

For mine eyes have seen thy salvation,

Which thou hast prepared before the face of all people;

A light to lighten the Gentiles, and the glory of thy people Israel.

And Joseph and his mother marvelled at those things which were spoken of him.

*The Presentation*
*in the Temple*
from an anonymous
Book of Hours

Eus in adiu
torium meū
ntende

*The Adoration of the Magi*
attributed to Raffaello Botticini

Now when Jesus was born in Bethlehem of Judaea in the days of Herod the king, behold, there came wise men from the east to Jerusalem,

Saying, Where is he that is born King of the Jews? for we have seen his star in the east, and are come to worship him.

When Herod the king had heard these things, he was troubled, and all Jerusalem with him.

And when he had gathered all the chief priests and scribes of the people together, he demanded of them where Christ should be born.

And they said unto him, In Bethlehem of Judaea: for thus it is written by the prophet,

And thou Bethlehem, in the land of Juda, art not the least among the princes of Juda: for out of thee shall come a Governor, that shall rule my people Israel.

THEN Herod, when he had privily called the wise men, enquired of them diligently what time the star appeared.

And he sent them to Bethlehem, and said, Go and search diligently for the young child; and when ye have found him, bring me word again, that I may come and worship him also.

When they had heard the king, they departed; and, lo, the star, which they saw in the east, went before them, till it came and stood over where the young child was.

When they saw the star, they rejoiced with exceeding great joy.

And when they were come into the house, they saw the young child with Mary his mother, and fell down, and worshipped him.

*The Adoration of the Magi*
attributed to Jan van Scorel

And when they had opened their treasures, they presented unto him gifts; gold, and frankincense, and myrrh. And being warned of God in a dream that they should not return to Herod, they departed into their own country another way.

*The Adoration of the Magi* by a follower of Lucas van Leyden

AND when they were departed, behold, the angel of the Lord appeareth to Joseph in a dream, saying, Arise, and take the young child and his mother, and flee into Egypt, and be thou there until I bring thee word: for Herod will seek the young child to destroy him.

When he arose, he took the young child and his mother by night, and departed into Egypt:

And was there until the death of Herod: that it might be fulfilled which was spoken of the Lord by the prophet, saying, Out of Egypt have I called my son.

Then Herod, when he saw that he was mocked of the wise men, was exceeding wroth, and sent forth, and slew all the children that were in Bethlehem, and in all the coasts thereof, from two years old and under, according to the time which he had diligently enquired of the wise men.

But when Herod was dead, behold, an angel of the Lord appeareth in a dream to Joseph in Egypt,

Saying, Arise, and take the young child and his mother, and go into the land of Israel: for they are dead which sought the young child's life.

And he arose, and took the young child and his mother, and came into the land of Israel.

But when he heard that Archelaus did reign in Judaea in the room of his father Herod, he was afraid to go thither: notwithstanding, being warned of God in a dream, he turned aside into the parts of Galilee:

And he came and dwelt in a city called Nazareth: that it might be fulfilled which was spoken by the prophets, He shall be called a Nazarene.

*The Flight into Egypt*
by Bernardino Butinone

AND the child grew,
and waxed strong in spirit,
filled with wisdom:
and the grace of God
was upon him.

*Virgin and Child Crowned by Angels* by Colyn de Coter

# Checklist of Works

**Anonymous Book of Hours** (French)
*The Presentation in the Temple*, c. 1470
Illumination on vellum; 6¾ x 4¾ in.
Gift of Sarah Raymond Fitzwilliam, 1917.796; Ill. p. 27

**Anonymous Book of Hours** (French)
*The Annunciation to the Shepherds*, c. 1470
Illumination on vellum; 6¾ x 4¾ in.
Gift of Sarah Raymond Fitzwilliam, 1917.796; Ill. p. 20

**Anonymous** (German)
*The Nativity* from *The Spicegarden of the Soul*, 1483
Woodcut on paper; 7¾ x 5 in.
Gift of Mrs. Potter Palmer, 1947.438; Ill. p. 24

**Sandro Botticelli** (Italian, 1444/1445–1510)
*Virgin and Child with Angel*, 1475/85
Tempera on panel; 33¾ x 23¼ in.
Max and Leola Epstein Collection, 1954.283; Ill. frontispiece

**Attributed to Raffaello Botticini** (Italian, 1477–c. 1520)
*The Adoration of the Magi*, c. 1495
Tempera on panel; diam. 41 in.
Mr. and Mrs. Martin A. Ryerson Collection, 1937.997;
Ill. pp. 28–29

**Bernardino Butinone** (Italian, active 1484–1507)
*The Flight into Egypt*, c. 1485
Tempera on panel, 10⅛ x 8⅜ in.
Mr. and Mrs. Martin A. Ryerson Collection, 1933.1003;
Ill. p. 35

**Colyn de Coter** (Netherlandish, c. 1450/1455–before
1539/1540)
*Virgin and Child Crowned by Angels*, 1490/1510
Oil on panel; 59⅞ x 34⅞ in.
Mr. and Mrs. Martin A. Ryerson Collection, 1933.1039;
Ill. pp. 36–37

**Lucas Cranach the Elder** (German, 1472–1553)
*Angel* from *The Wittenberg Book of Reliquaries*, 1509
Woodcut on paper; 7⅝ x 5½ in.
Clarence Buckingham Collection, 1948.111; Ill. p. 6

**Bartolommeo di Giovanni** (Italian, c. 1465–1501)
*Scenes from the Life of Saint John the Baptist*, 1490/95
Tempera on panel; 29¼ x 59¼ in.
Mr. and Mrs. Martin A. Ryerson Collection, 1937.996;
Ill. pp. 12, 14–15

**Jean Hey** (The Master of Moulins, French, active
c. 1490/1510)
*The Annunciation*, c. 1500
Oil on panel; 28⅜ x 19¾ in.
Mr. and Mrs. Martin A. Ryerson Collection, 1933.1062;
Ill. pp. 8–9

**Johann Koerbecke** (German, c. 1420–1491)
*The Annunciation*, completed by 1457
Oil on panel, transferred to canvas; 36¾ x 25⅞ in.
Mr. and Mrs. Martin A. Ryerson Collection, 1933.1064;
Ill. p. 11

**Follower of Lucas van Leyden** (Netherlandish,
1494–1538)
*The Adoration of the Magi*, c. 1510
Oil on panel; 11¼ x 14 in.
Mr. and Mrs. Martin A. Ryerson Collection, 1933.1045;
Ill. pp. 32–33

**Master of the Historia Friderici et Maximiliani**
(Austrian, active c. 1510–1520)
*The Nativity*, 1511/12
Oil on panel; 44 x 29¼ in.
Wilson L. Mead Fund, 1933.799; Ill. pp. 16–17

**Jacob Cornelisz. van Oostsanen** (Netherlandish,
c. 1470–1533)
*The Adoration of the Christ Child*, c. 1520
Oil on panel; 38⅞ x 30⅛ in.
George F. Harding Collection, 1983.375; Ill. pp. 22–23, 25

**Pietro di Cristoforo Vannucci, called Perugino** (Italian,
1445/46–1523)
*The Adoration of the Christ Child*, 1500/05
Tempera on panel, transferred to canvas; 10⅜ x 18¼ in.
Mr. and Mrs. Martin A. Ryerson Collection, 1933.1025;
Ill. pp. 18–19

**Peter Paul Rubens** (Flemish, 1577–1640)
*The Adoration of the Eucharist*, c. 1626
Oil on panel; 12½ x 12½ in.
Mr. and Mrs. Martin A. Ryerson Collection, 1937.1012;
Ill. p. 5

**Attributed to Jan van Scorel** (Netherlandish, 1495–1562)
*The Adoration of the Magi*, 1519/20
Oil on panel; 17⅝ x 21¾ in.
Wilson L. Mead Fund, 1935.381; Ill. pp. 30–31

The Art Institute of Chicago Publications Department
Susan F. Rossen, Executive Director

Edited by Adam Jolles
Production by Katherine Houck Fredrickson,
assisted by Manine Rosa Golden

Design and typography by Lynn Martin Design, Chicago
Color separations by Elite Color Group, Providence, Rhode Island
Printed by Meridian Printing, East Greenwich, Rhode Island

Photographs by the Department of Imaging and Technical Services
Alan B. Newman, Executive Director

Unless otherwise noted, all biblical text is excerpted from the Gospels
of Luke and Matthew in the King James Bible

The following illustrations were reprinted from *The Illustrated Bartsch*,
©1981 by Abaris Books, Inc., 42 Memorial Plaza, Pleasantville, N.Y. 10570:
p. 10: *The Annunciation* (v. 81, no. 1476/79)
p. 13: *The Visitation* (v. 87, no. 1487/6)
p. 21: *The Annunciation to the Shepherds* (v. 81, no. 1476/87)
p. 26: *The Presentation in the Temple* (v. 83, no. 1481/294)
p. 34: *The Massacre of the Innocents* (v. 83, no. 1481/498)